Anecdotes Of The Stage: Or Dramatic Table Talk In Theatrical History And Biography

James G. Bertram

In the interest of creating a more extensive selection of rare historical book reprints, we have chosen to reproduce this title even though it may possibly have occasional imperfections such as missing and blurred pages, missing text, poor pictures, markings, dark backgrounds and other reproduction issues beyond our control. Because this work is culturally important, we have made it available as a part of our commitment to protecting, preserving and promoting the world's literature. Thank you for your understanding.

ANECDOTES OF THE STAGE.

FOOTIANA.

WE have extracted the following anecdotes and bon mots of the English Aristophanes from a scarce pamphlet obtained by the kindness of a friend, entitled Memoirs of the Life and Writings of Samuel Foote, Esq. (Bew, Paternoster Row, 1777.) As a memoir, the book is worthless; eulogy is not history; but, as it contains many *theatrical facts* it is valuable. The few anecdotes we have extracted, will not be found among the hackneyed ones that bear his name.

Foote, in all his pieces, where he has introduced a Scotchman, has been very severe on that nation; it was from no antipathy he had to them, but jokes more readily sprang up from satire than panegyric, and he was one of that sort, that he would rather lose his friend than his jest. In the Devil upon Two Sticks, where two physicians are discoursing together, the one Scotch and the other Irish, a stander-by asks if botany is not a dry study in Scotland; to which the Irishman replies, "To be sure it is, for they have nothing but dried herbs; the devil a green one will grow there. Why, all their cabbages are thistles, and even those they raise in hot beds."

When Foote heard of Sir Francis Blake Delaval's death, the shock of losing so intimate a friend had such an effect on his spirits, that he burst into tears, retired to his room, and saw no company for two days: the third day, Jewel, his treasurer, calling in upon him, he asked him, with swollen eyes, what time would the burial be. "Not till next week, sir," replied the other, "as I hear the surgeons are first to dissect his *head*." This last word recovered the wit's fancy, and repeating it with some surprise, he asked, "And what the devil will they get there? I am sure," says he, "I have known poor Frank these five-and-twenty years, and I never could find *any thing* in it."

When Mr Foote's piece of the Minor was first brought out, some of the clergy took umbrage at a passage in it, which Mrs Cole speaks, viz., "had it not been for him, I had been a lost sheep," saying, that it was wrong to introduce any part of the scriptures on the stage in buffoonery. The play was then performing, consequently had received the approbation of the chamberlain. The bishop of London, it is said, sent for Mr Foote, and remonstrated with him on the impropriety; Foote assured his lordship it should be altered on the next representation, which was accordingly done; for when he came to that line, he said, "had it not been for him, I had been a lost *mutton*."

Foote being one night very merry at the Bedford coffee-house, the conversation happened to turn on the abilities of Mr Garrick as an actor, when, amongst many compliments to that celebrated performer, it was observed as somewhat extraordinary, that though he was so excellent an actor himself, he was far from being lucky in his pupils. "Why, yes," replies Foote, "he is something like the famous running-horse Childers; the best racer in England *himself*, but could *never get a colt*."

When Foote first heard of Doctor Blair's writing notes to Ossian, (a performance, the *reality* of which has been doubted,) he observed that the booksellers ought to allow a great discount to the purchasers. "Why so," says a gentleman present. "Because," says he, "they are *notes* of enormous *long credit*."

At the time of the Jubilee at Stratford, planned and conducted by Mr Garrick, in honour of Shakespeare, the weather in general (though early in September) turned out very bad; particularly the day appointed for the public procession, which obliged that part of the ceremony to be dispensed with. Garrick meeting Foote on the morning of this day in the public breakfasting-room, just in the moment of a very heavy shower of rain, "Well, Sam," says he, rather disappointedly, "what do you think of this?" "Think of it," says Foote, "why, I think, it is *God's revenge against vanity*."

Foote and the Delavals being out one night playing their pranks, and kicking up a dust, got into a squabble at a house of ill fame, and were going to throw the landlady out of the window, after having demolished a number of bowls and other china ware.. A constable was sent for, and they were carried before Sir Thomas De Veil, who was then the acting justice for Westminster. Though Foote and his companions were well known to the justice, had they been called by their names, yet he was a stranger to their persons; he began to harangue them harshly. "Come," says he, "good woman," to the landlady, "stand *before* me, and tell your story." "Aye, do," says Foote, "tell the truth, and *face* the *Devil*," pointing with his hat to Sir Thomas. However, the justice, on hearing their names, settled the matter, and discharged the culprits.

Foote being at supper one night at the Bedford coffee-house, just after Garrick had performed Macbeth, the conversation very naturally turned on the merits of that great performer; when, after many eulogiums on the universality of his powers, it was allowed that he was the first actor *on* any *stage*. "Indeed, gentlemen," says Foote, "I do not think you have said *half* enough of him, for I think him not only the *greatest* actor *on*, but *off** the stage."

Mr Foote being asked his opinion of the Stratford Jubilee, replied, "A Jubilee is a public invitation, urged by puffing, to go post without horses to an obscure borough without representatives; governed by a mayor and aldermen, who are no magistrates; to celebrate a great poet, whose own works have made him immortal, by an ode without poetry; music without melody; a dinner without victuals; lodgings without beds; a crowd without company; a masquerade where half the people appeared bare-faced; a horse-race up to the knees in water; fire-works extinguished as soon as they were lighted; and a boarded booth, by way of amphitheatre, which was to be taken down in three days, and sold by public auction."

Mr Foote walking up and down the rooms at Bath, a gentleman with him asked a third a lady's name just then passing by them; to which he replied, "Brown, sir." "Aye," says Foote, staring at the lady, "a lovely *Brown* indeed!"

---

* It was from this hint, perhaps, Dr Goldsmith took the idea of Garrick's character, in his poem called Retaliation.

When Foote was told of Doctor B———n's death, he said he had cut his throat, to prove (multum in parvo) the rectitude of all his conclusions upon the manners and principles of the times, being the sum total of all his *theoretical divisions*, reduced to this single and concise rule of practice.

One day, where the wit was in company, the building of Richmond Bridge was the topic; a gentleman asked what the piers were to be built of, wood or stone. "Stone, to be sure," says Foote, "for there are too many *wooden peers* already in this country."

Foote some time ago took a house at Hammersmith that was advertised to be *completely furnished*. But he had not been there long, before the cook complained there was never a rolling-pin. "No," said he, "then bring me a saw, I will soon make one." Which he accordingly did of one of the mahogany bed-posts. The next day it was discovered there wanted a coal-scuttle; and he supplied this deficiency with a drawer from a curious japan chest of drawers. There was never a carpet in the parlour, and he ordered a new white cotton counterpane to be laid to save the boards. His landlord paying him a visit to inquire how he liked his new residence, was greatly astonished to find such disorder, as he considered it: he remonstrated to Mr Foote, and complained of the injury his furniture had sustained; but the genius insisted upon it, all the complaint was on his side, considering the trouble he had been at to supply those necessaries, notwithstanding he had advertised his house *completely furnished*. The landlord now threatened the law; and Foote threatened to take him off, saying, an auctioneer was a fruitful character. This last consideration weighed with the landlord, and he quietly put up with his loss.

Mr Foote was once asked why learned men are to be found in rich men's houses, and rich men never to be seen in those of the learned. "Why," says he, "the first know what they want, but the latter do not."

In all the disputes Foote used to have about the literature of Scotland, he never would allow that any of them were deeply learned. "I'll allow you," says he, "they all have a *mouthful* of learning, but not one of them has a *bellyful*."

Foote having satirised the Scotch pretty severely, a gentleman asked "Why he hated that nation so much." "You are mistaken," says Foote, "I don't hate the Scotch, neither do I hate frogs, but I would have everything keep to its *native element*."

EARLY THEATRICALS IN EDINBURGH.

THE origin of plays in Edinburgh is involved in great obscurity, and the history of the drama in the metropolis of Scotland is one of fitful encouragement and meagre results; the patronage of royalty being hardly sufficient, at one time, to protect it from the ignominious expulsion so ardently desired by the early reformers, who were loud in their denunciations against it.

In the earlier stages of its history are to be found various notices of religious theatrical representations, performed principally by parties of domestics, and originating evidently in the church. The first approach to regular dramatic composition after this period was Sir David Lindsay's "Pleasant Satyre of the Three Estatis," a piece, which, we are told by Charteris, was performed in 1544 before the Queen Regent, and which so far surpasses the efforts of contemporary English dramatists as to render the barrenness of the Scottish muse in this department of literature afterwards the more apparent. James VI. was fond of this kind of amusement, and issued a mandate to his clergy to drop their censures of theatrical representations, which at certain periods during his reign they used periodically to anathematize. The civil wars in the reign of Charles I., and the gloomy fanaticism which spread itself among the people, left neither leisure nor inclination for the intellectual amusements of the stage, and the striking changes that then occurred almost obliterated all trace of theatrical representations until after the Restoration. In the early days of acting, the players were attached to the household of the King, or his brother, the Duke of York. They also wore a kind of uniform or livery, and were termed respectively *the King's* or *the Duke's servants*, and in that character they were followers of the courts of the king, or of the duke, their master; and in this situation we accordingly find a party of them at Holyrood with the Duke of York in the year 1680, no doubt contributing greatly to the amusement of the court and the courtiers.

The misfortunes attending the duke's journey on his return to England, the political fever of his reign, and the sullen bigotry into which that fever subsided in the time of his successor, once more dissipated so effectually all ideas of polite or rational amusement, that no return of the drama is to be traced in Scotland, even in the reign of Queen Anne, the Augustan age of her sister country; and it was not until after the ferment excited by the Union, and the confusion attendant on the memorable rebellion of 1715 had subsided, that any stage-players thought of venturing a trial of fortune in the Modern Athens.

The first of these was Signora Violante, an Italian posture mistress, celebrated for feats of strength, and whom Arnot describes as "a virago." She fitted up a temporary theatre at the bottom of Carrubber's Close, and collected a company of English comedians, who met with much encouragement from such portion of the inhabitants as were play-goers. For some years after this period, a company of strollers annually visited Edinburgh. From a certain quarter, however, they met with great opposition, the clergy having a most illiberal and violent animosity against the stage, the players, and the eloquence that

"Stirs the blood and fires the brain."

So lately as in the year 1727, the Magistrates and Presbytery of Edinburgh endeavoured to expel the comedians from the boundaries of the city. However, notwithstanding the active fulminations of the clergy and magistrates, the players held their ground, and continued to act in the very teeth of their opposition. The itinerant companies who at this period visited the city, having been driven from their stronghold in Carrubber's Close, usually rented the Taylor's Hall in the Cowgate, which they fitted up as a temporary theatre; the prices of admission were, for the boxes and pit, 2s. 6d.; and for the Gallery, 1s. 6d. The clergy again assailed and preached against "the house of the Devil" more bitterly than ever, but it was not without its defenders; and the Professors of the College, and several of the most respectable inhabitants, came forward to support the players thus persecuted into popularity. A spirit of party was thus engendered, which became of great benefit to the success of the "Theatre," and so great did the attendance become, that the Taylor's Hall was soon found to be insufficient to accommodate the numerous spectators.

During this brief glimpse of prosperity the company differed among themselves; and a factious performer having engaged in his party the late Mrs Ward, then in the bloom of her youth and beauty, attempted to ruin the manager of Taylor's Hall, by setting up a rival house. An area was pitched upon to the west of St John Street, Canongate, and the foundation-stone laid in August 1746, by Mr John Ryan of Covent Garden, an actor of distinguished merit. No sooner were the doors opened, than the Taylor's Hall was deserted, and the manager ruined. The success of the new house was for one season greatly enhanced by the following circumstance:—One Robert Drummond, a printer, had been sentenced by the magistrates to be pilloried, and banished the city for a twelvemonth, for printing a defamatory poem, or libel, reflecting upon the Duke of Cumberland, and certain zealous Whigs. His printing-house being shut up, and his journeymen and apprentices set idle in consequence of the sentence, it was contrived that the pastoral comedy of the *Gentle Shepherd* should be acted by these journeymen and apprentices for the behoof of their distressed master. As the sentence against Drummond was deemed rigorous, and as it had become a party affair, the scheme of a play was wonderfully relished, and the play repeatedly performed before such crowded houses, that it was found necessary to erect occasional galleries over the stage for the convenience of spectators.

The Canongate Theatre, under the management of Mr Lee, soon began to get into difficulties, with which the manager contrived to struggle for a considerable period, bringing down various performers of merit from London, in order, if possible, to get the theatre out of debt. This method, however, only added to his liabilities, and the theatre speedily changed hands. Some of the members of the College of Justice having been security for Mr Lee's debts, the property fell into their hands, and they appointing a Mr James Callender, merchant in Edinburgh, to act for them, the celebrated actor Digges, who was then at Dublin, was engaged as stage-manager. Lee, of course, complained heavily of these proceedings. He insisted that the conveyance granted by him was merely a mode of security, not a deed of sale: that he had been imposed upon as to the form of the writ, and taken advantage of in the price for the subject, which was no more than L.500, while the property was truly worth L.1700. To obtain redress of his grievances, Mr Lee brought an action before the Court of Session, and a party was formed to oppose the new managers. After two or three pleadings the action was dropped, and Mr Digges' figure and address defeated the opposition.

The extension of Edinburgh by the projection of the New Town soon rendered the old part of the city an unfavourable spot for the prosperity of the theatre, and, in accordance with the advancing spirit of the times, a royal patent was secured for a house to be built in the modern part of the city. The first holder of the patent was a Mr Ross, at that time a "principal performer" at Covent Garden, who secured this privilege by paying off some old debts, amounting to £1100, incurred by the gentlemen who had formerly taken an interest in "the old town concern," who in this manner were very glad to get out of a pecuniary scrape into which their fondness for theatrical amusements had unwarily drawn them.

Mr Ross, being in possession of the patent, set about the erection of a suitable building, which, it is scarcely necessary to say, is the present barn-like edifice, which produces the double effect of disgusting spectators by its own deformity, and obstructing the view of one of the finest buildings in the empire. Mr Ross being, like a great many of the members of his profession, a poor man, had some difficulty in the devising ways and means of raising money to defray the expense of the proposed edifice. The mode ultimately resorted to was a proposition to raise £2500 in so many shares of £100 each, security being given on the building, the patent, the wardrobe, scenery, machinery, &c., &c. Each share was to pay three per cent. of interest to the holder, besides giving a privilege of free admission upon all occasions of the building being open. The building was commenced in 1768, and the house was opened in December 1769, at a total expense of about £5000. The prices of admission were—three shillings to the pit and boxes, two shillings to the lower gallery, and one shilling to the upper one. At these rates the house held about £140 sterling, being nearly double the sum which the Canongate theatre held.

The falling of the North Bridge was a great blow to the

theatre. At one fell swoop it cut off the best communication between the populous districts of old Edinburgh and the, at that time, scantily populated New Town, containing the temple of the drama. The indifference of the company, too, gave little inducement to people to put themselves out of the way to visit a house of entertainment so difficult of access. The manager exclaimed loudly, in his own defence, that good actors, in consequence of the fall of the bridge, would not engage with him. Be that as it may, however, his campaign was a very unsuccessful one. We suspect he trusted too much to the novelty of the mere building, and neglected the one grand and first requisite of success as a theatrical manager— the gathering together of a first-rate company.

The theatre was now a legalised entertainment in Edinburgh. It was only, however, in December 1767, that the establishment was placed under the protection of the law, and on that occasion a prologue, suited to the occasion, was delivered by Mr Ross, in which the royal grant was thus noticed:—

"This night lov'd George's free enlightened age
Bids *royal favour* shield the Scottish stage.
His Royal favour ev'ry bosom cheers;
The drama now with dignity appears."

Mr Ross soon tired of his managerial cares; and, in a fit of disgust and disappointment, he let the theatre for three years to Mr Foote. That gentleman engaged a first-rate company, and the result was, that, after paying all expenses, he was the gainer at the end of the season of a clear £1000. But, Foote having concerns of more importance in London, to which it was necessary he should devote his whole attention, speedily retired from the management, and gave over his lease to Messrs Digges and Bland, who had possession of it for some years. It was afterwards rented by Mr Corrie, then by Mr Wilkinson, and afterwards by Mr John Jackson, the historian of the Scottish stage.

This gentleman got possession on November 10, 1781. He put the house into a thorough state of repair, furnished it anew with scenery, ornaments, properties, and wardrobe. His resident company of performers was also first-rate, and, under his management, the citizens had the gratification of seeing Mrs Siddons, Mrs Jordan, and the other unrivalled *artistes* of the day. As a contrast to the grandiloquent managerial puffs of the present time we take the liberty of giving Mr Jackson's address:—

"TO THE PUBLIC.

"I do myself the honour of seizing the earliest opportunity of informing the ladies and gentlemen of the city of Edinburgh that the superintendence of the Theatre-Royal has at length fallen to my lot. The task is always arduous, and in the present instance rendered still more difficult from the shortness of the time allowed me for the necessary preparations for the season, my agreement with Mr Ross for the purchase of the theatre not having been concluded till the 10th of the present month. Even with this additional inconvenience, I embrace the situation with pleasure. Naturalised, as it were, by inclination and a long residence in Scotland, I cannot help looking forward with a glow of satisfaction on an appointment which flatters me with a pleasing expectation of passing the latter part of my life in a country, for which, from my earliest years, I have ever entertained the strongest attachment. The difficulties I must necessarily at present encounter, shall be combated by an unremitted perseverance. As a servant of the public, I shall think myself bound, on all occasions, to make my opinion subservient to their wishes. A predilection to representations that exhibit those moral principles that the stage was intended to promote, and a constant endeavour to procure the most capital performers that can be had, to fill the various characters, shall claim my first attention in the appointment of every theatrical exhibition," &c., &c.

"JOHN JACKSON."

Most of the great performers of the day were engaged by Mr Jackson. Among others, Mrs Jordan, Mr Pope and Mrs Pope, Mrs Kennedy, "the celebrated singer," Mr Lee Lewes, Mr Fennell, Mrs Percy, Mr King, Miss Farren, Miss Kemble, Mr John Kemble, and many more whom we have not space to enumerate. It may be interesting to our readers if we present them with some idea of the financial state of the theatre during Mr Jackson's management. Thus in 1789, the income amounted to - - - - £5180 5 0

While the expenditure was 4454 1 5

Leaving a profit of £726 3 7

In 1790, the income is stated at - £5275 8 6
The expenses are reckoned at - 5297 1 11

Leaving in that year a loss of £21 18 5

The weekly expenses to performers amounted, in 1790, to £100, 8s.; and the sum put down for lights, music, servants, fees, &c., &c., is £60, 5s. Mr Jackson also paid out a great many large sums for repairs, painting, scenery, machinery, &c., in order to make the house as complete and perfect as possible.

Towards the end of his period of management, it would seem that Mr Jackson had got into difficulties, and it was resolved that Mr Stephen Kemble, the eminent provincial manager, should be associated in the management, on the condition of paying a rent of £1300, and giving Mr Jackson half the profits. Mr Kemble, at the same time, to have a salary for his services as manager.

The following is a list of the permanent company engaged by Mr Foote in 1771 :—

Mr Foote,	Mr Robson,
... Woodward,	... Miller,
... Weston,	... Waker,
... Sowdon,	... Bain,
... Jackson,	... Knowles,
... Vendermore,	... Vowell,
... Lancashire,	... Farrel,
... Didier,	... Dancer,
... Gentleman,	... Maurell,
... Fearon,	... Collins.
Mrs Baker,	Mrs Waker,
... Jackson	... Fearon,
... Jewel,	... Farrel,
... Didier,	... Collins.

List of the company performing in Edinburgh in 1790 under Mr Jackson :—

Mr King,	Mr Hallion,
... Pope,	... Bell,
... Wilson,	... Bland, senior,
... Wood,	... Bland, junior,
... Lamash,	... J. Bland,
... Moss,	... Charteris,

Mr Williamson,	Mr Charteris, junior,
... Archer,	... Sparks,
... Taylor,	... Woodroffe,
... Lowe,	... Bonville,
... Mapples,	... Mountfort.
... Jackson,	

Mrs Esten,	Mrs Lowe,
... Barresforde,	... Clarke,
... Taylor,	... Charteris,
... W. Wells,	... Archer,
... Sparks,	... Mountfort,
... Woods,	... Bland,
... Jackson,	Miss Fontenelle.

After the agreement between Jackson and Kemble had expired, the latter gentleman resolved upon commencing a new establishment solely on his own account. With this view, he fitted up the Circus, and engaged the following ladies and gentlemen as members of the new theatre:—

Mr Kemble,	Mr Edwin,
... Lee Lewes,	... Bell,
... Woods,	... Sparks,
... Archer,	... Whitmore,
... Swendal,	... Moreton,
... Fox,	... Clark,
... C. Kemble,	... Ruberry,
... Siddons, junior,	... Crew.
... Price,	

Mrs Kemble,	Mrs Walcott,
... Lee Lewes,	... Edwin,
... Woods,	Miss Ross,
... Ruberry,	... Satchell.

Kemble opened on the 21st January 1793; Jackson's friends, of course, went to law in defence of his patent. The Lord Ordinary interdicted Kemble, and he reclaimed against the interdict, but the Lords determined against the New Theatre, and "by this decree," says Jackson, "the Theatre-Royal was established in its natural and ancient privileges, and once more opened with the fulness of its powers."— LIFE OF MURRAY.

KEMBLE AND MATHEWS.

When Kemble retired from the stage he distributed his costume of *Coriolanus* amongst his brethren. To Mathews he gave his sandals, upon which the comedian exclaimed, "I'm glad I've got his sandals, for I am sure I could never *tread in his shoes.*"

SHERIDAN.

This celebrated wit once said to Erskine, "Ah, Tom, had I stuck to the law, I might have been what you are; but, curse it, Mrs S. or myself were always obliged to write for our daily *leg* or *shoulder* of mutton." "Ah!" said Erskine, "I always heard your literature was a *joint* concern."

SIR ROBERT WALPOLE.

Although Sir Robert Walpole was frequently the subject of Gay's satire, yet this did not deter him from attending the performance of the Beggars' Opera. He was in one of the stage boxes at its first representation, when an universal *encore* attended the following air, which is sung by Lockit :—

"When you censure the age
Be cautious and sage,
Lest the courtiers offended should be;
If you mention *vice* or *bribe*,
'Tis so pat to all the tribe,
That each cries, *this was levelled at me.*"

While this air was repeating, all eyes were directed to the minister; and Sir Robert observing the pointed manner in which the audience applied the last line to him, parried the hit by encoring it a second time with his single voice; and thus not only blunted the poetical shaft, but gained a general huzza from the audience. Few pieces ever met with such decided success as the Beggars' Opera, which was performed sixty-three nights the first season, and is still a great favourite on the stage.

THE EDINBURGH THEATRE DURING THE REBELLION.

AFTER the Rebellion of 1745, the divided spectators frequently displayed in the theatre a spirit of political dissention. Upon the anniversary of the battle of Culloden, 1749, this animosity rose to a height which threatened consequences of a serious nature. Certain military gentlemen who were in the playhouse called out to the band of music to play *Culloden*.* This was regarded by the audience as ungenerously and insolently upbraiding the country with her misfortunes. Resenting it, accordingly, they ordered the band to play, *You're welcome, Charles Stuart*.† The musicians complying, instantly a number of officers attacked the orchestra with drawn swords, and leaped upon the stage. Among them was the son of a chieftian, who had drawn the Pretender on to his rash attempt, by offering to join him with his clan, and who, upon the Prince's landing, raised his clan, it is true; but, instead of fulfilling his engagements, joined the royal army. This young gentleman, leaping upon the stage, to display the zealousness of his loyalty, slipped his foot, and fell flat upon the stage. The spectators being tickled with the circumstance, an immense peal of laughter burst through the house, which exasperated the indignation of the officers. Meantime, fiddlesticks being unable to cope with polished steel, the musicians fled; but the military were not long able to remain masters of the field. They were assailed from the galleries with apples, snuff-boxes, broken forms, in short, with everything missile that could be laid hold of. The officers at once consulted their safety, and went in quest of revenge by quitting the stage, in order to attack the galleries, which they stormed, sword in hand. The inhabitants of these upper regions defended themselves from the fury of the soldiers by barricading their doors. The Highland chairmen, learning the nature of the quarrel, with their poles, attacked the officers in the rear, who, being neither able to advance nor retreat, were obliged to surrender

---

* A tune composed in order to keep up the remembrance of the bloody defeat of an unfortunate party.
† A song of the Jacobite party.

at discretion, leaving the chairmen masters of the field. Luckily, no misfortune of any consequence happened in this fray; and to prevent similar disturbances, bills were next day pasted up, wherein it was notified, in large rubrics, that, for the future, the band of music was not to play any tunes at the desire of the audience, but select pieces appointed by the managers.—LIFE OF W. H. MURRAY.

INCLEDON AND THE HORSE.

SUETT the comedian, familiarly called "Dicky Suett," one day meeting Incledon at Tattersall's, asked him if he had come to buy a horse. Incledon said he had; but having no opinion of Suett's judgment in horse flesh, inquired—" What do you do here? Do you think you should know a horse from an ass?" "No doubt," replied Suett quietly, "I'd engage to pick you out among a thousand horses."

THEATRICAL SOCIETY IN EDINBURGH—1816-22.

THE Edinburgh Theatre at this period was worth a visit. Sir Walter Scott who gave the tone to the literary society for which Edinburgh is so famed, often led his friends to Shakespeare Square, to be amused with the drolleries of Will Murray. Hogg, J. G. Lockhart, Professor Wilson, and the Ballantynes, and many other critics whose words were law to both author and actor, nightly graced the house. Sir Walter had a warm and affectionate feeling to Mr Murray, and has often spoken of him with great kindness and regard. The Ballantynes, both John and James, were excellent critics, and they undoubtedly exercised a considerable degree of influence on Theatrical matters in Edinburgh. Mr John Ballantyne, in particular, took a warm personal interest in the success of the Theatre under Mr Murray, and was the friend and adviser of many an actor who has since risen to affluence. The inimitable Mathew's was indebted to him for some of his best stories, and for many hints as to his entertainments, and, in fact, " whatever actor or singer of eminance visited Edinburgh of the evenings when he did not perform, several were sure to be reserved for Trinity, (Mr John Ballantyne's Villa). Here Braham quavered, and here Liston drolled his best—here Johnstone and Murray and Yates mixed jest and stave—here Kean revelled and rioted—and here the Roman Kemble often played the Greek, from sunset to dawn. Nor did the popular *cantatrice* or *danseuse* of the time disdain to freshen her roses after a laborious week amidst these Paphian arbours of Harmony Hall."

MISS FOOTE.

This lady told a comedian that she thought no pleasure surpassed that of rapid travelling. "I must differ from you, madam," said he, "for I should think no pleasure so great as to travel on *foot.*"

PIZARRO.

A LADY, speaking of this play, said, "How beautiful in that scene when all the virgins range themselves, each with a *little sun* at her breast." This is very well in a theatre, but having *a little son at the breast* might endanger the virgin character elsewhere.

ROB ROY.

THE great salvation of the concern (the Edinburgh Theatre), was the never-to-be-forgotten *Rob Roy*, which brought to the treasury a sum of £3000, and which has been played about 300 times in the Edinburgh Theatre-Royal since its first production. So great was the sensation excited by it, that long after the run of the piece was over, and a few bad houses intervening, *Rob Roy* would draw a £60 house at any time.—MURRAY'S LIFE.

LITTLE KNIGHT.

When this actor led his second lady to the altar, Tate Wilkinson said to her, "I wish you joy on your wedding-day, madam, but I lament that you'll have but a *short night.*"

STAGE FEELING.

King has recorded of Garrick, that whilst that great actor was drowning the house in tears, in the fourth act of Lear, he put his tongue in his cheek, and said to him, during the applause, "D——n me, Tom, it will do, it will do."

MRS HENRY SIDDONS.

In the end of 1844, died Mrs Henry Siddons, who, for upwards of twenty-five years, was the distinguished luminary of the Edinburgh Theatre, of which valuable property she eventually became nearly the sole proprietor. During that long period, Mrs Siddons not only delighted the Edinburgh audience by her own fascinating personations, but in conjunction with her accomplished brother, our present worthy manager, gave a tone of refinement to our dramatic representations, and of high respectability to the profession, which elevated the character of our stage. In the higher walk of comedy, we believe, Mrs H. Siddons was admitted to be surpassed by none on the metropolitan boards, even in that bright era. As *Beatrice, Rosalind, Portia, Lady Teazle, Miss Hardcastle,* and a long list which it would be impossible to enumerate here, few will forget the style of her acting. It was comic vivacity of the highest order; playful, brilliant, and full of exquisite point and polish, though Mrs Siddons could impart deep interest to scenes of quiet pathos—and we retain a vivid recollection of her efforts in some of her best melo-dramas and short dramatic sketches—still she did not aspire to the more impassioned and lofty sphere of the drama. Her style was the beautiful, not the grand, which she willingly resigned to her great relative, whose name she so willingly bore. But in her own province—and it can scarcely be said to be secondary to, but rather co-ordinate with the strict domain of the tragic muse—Mrs Siddons stood almost alone in excellence. In private life, Mrs Siddons was the model of all that was exemplary and amiable, pursuing the tenor of her domestic duties, contemporaneously with professional toil, with a quiet undeviating care, that rendered her no less beloved in her immediate circle than admired in the dramatic scene. By a numerous and most select circle of private friends, the loss of this lady was deeply felt, such was her modest unassuming grace in society, and the public will long associate her memory with many of their most delightful and intellectual hours of recreation.—LIFE OF MURRAY.

BENEFIT PLAY-BILL.

LINTON, a musician belonging to the orchestra of Covent Garden Theatre, was murdered by some street robbers, who were discovered and executed. A play was given for the benefit of his widow and children, and the day preceding the performance the following appeared in one of the public prints:—

Theatre-Royal, Covent Garden.

FOR THE BENEFIT OF MRS LINTON.

"That widow," said Charity, whispering in my ear, "must have your mite; wait upon her with a guinea, and purchase a box ticket."

"You may have one for five shillings," observed Avarice, pulling me by the elbow.

My hand was in my pocket, and the guinea which was between my fingers, sliped out.

"Yes," said I, "she shall have my five shillings."

"Good Heaven!" exclaimed Justice, "what are you about? Five Shillings! If you pay but five shillings for going into the theatre, then you get value received for your money."

"And I shall owe him no thanks," added Charity, laying

her hand upon my heart, and leading me on the way to the widow's house.

Taking the knocker in my left hand, my whole frame trembled. Looking round, I saw Avarice turn the corner of the street, and I found all the money in my pocket grasped in my hand.

"Is your mother at home, my dear," said I to a child, who conducted me into the parlour.

"Yes," answered the infant, "but my father has not been at home for a great while; that is his harpsichord, and that is his violin. He used to play on them for me."

"Shall I play you a tune, my boy?" said I.

"No, sir," continued the boy, "my mother will not let them be touched, for since my father went abroad, music makes her cry, and then we all cry."

I looked on the violin; it was unstrung. It was out of tune. Had the Lyre of Orpheus sounded in my ear, it could not have insinuated into my frame thrills of sensibility equal to what I felt.

"I hear my mother on the stairs," said the boy. I shook him by the hand. "Give her this," said I, and left the house. It rained; I called a coach, drove to a coffee-house, but not having a farthing in my pocket, borrowed a shilling at the bar.

THE TRAGEDY OF DOUGLAS AND THE EDINBURGH CLERGY.

THE production of the Rev. John Home's tragedy of *Douglas* was a great event in the history of the Theatre in Edinburgh. After the Presbyterian clergy had railed against the stage for upwards of a century and a half, it was a matter of no small mortification to them to behold a play written by one of their own order, acted in presence of several of their number, and received with universal applause. The tragedy was first performed in Edinburgh on the 14th December 1756. It was acted, for successive nights, before persons of all ranks and professions, and had a run unprecedented in the annals of any theatrical piece exhibited in Scotland. The presbytery at once took the alarm. They called before them such ministers within their district as had witnessed the performance of the play, and passed upon them a sentence of temporal suspension from the pastoral office. They, at the same time, wrote circular letters to those presbyteries in which any clergyman belonging to them had been present at the theatre, recommending rigorous proceedings against them. They went about to misrepresent the conduct of a certain clergyman, while in the play-house, interpreting into riotous behaviour a conduct that was, in all respects, manly, honourable, and decent. With regard to the play itself, they attacked it on account of its pretended irreligious and immoral tendency, alleging, in support of their charge, that there were certain impious invocations, or mock prayers, in it, and an expression of horrid swearing; besides that it encouraged suicide, and generally advancing all the cant and bigotted arguments usually put forth on such occasions. As to the author, he was cited to appear before his own presbytery, to answer the libel brought against him. But the poet, foreseeing the disagreeableness of his situation, and, perhaps, having no violent attachment to his profession, declined an appearance before his brethren, at the expense of resigning his pastoral charge. With respect to their flock, the presbytery drew up an *act and exhortation*, which was read from all the pulpits, and afterwards made its appearance in some periodical publications. In this address, the presbytery, after making the hackneyed complaint of the growth of immorality and irreligion, set forth, either from involuntary ignorance, or with deliberate falsehood, that the Christian had, in all ages, condemned dramatic representations—a circumstance not worth commenting on in this enlightened age, when all classes of the people have a proper appreciation of the elevating tendency which characterises the labours of the dramatist.—LIFE OF W. H. MURRAY.

MR AND MRS WEBB.

THIS worthy couple weighed at least sixteen stone each, and they once waited on Colman to complain of the smallness of their salaries. "Why, really, my poor fat people," says Colman, "*I have often wondered how you make both ends meet.*"

MACKLIN.

When he was rehearsing Macbeth, and, from want of memory, detained the performers uncommonly long at the theatre, one of them asked Shuter, if he did not think it very extraordinary, that a man so old, and infirm in intellects, should attempt such a character? Ned drily quoted from the play—

"The time has been,
That when the brains were out, the man would die,
And there an end :— but *now*—"

RIOT IN EDINBURGH ABOUT "HIGH LIFE BELOW STAIRS."

One of the greatest riots, with the exception of the celebrated O. P. Row, ever seen in a theatre, took place in that of Edinburgh, on the occasion of the production of *High Life below Stairs*. Although it is the province of the stage to lash the vices, and ridicule the follies of people in all ranks, yet, when this piece was brought out in Edinburgh, the footmen, taking it in high dudgeon that a farce reflecting on their fraternity should be exhibited, resolved that it should be no more performed. Accordingly, upon the second night of its being announced in the bills as a part of the entertainment, Mr Love, one of the managers, came upon the stage, and read a letter, containing the most violent threatenings, both against the actors and the house, in case the piece should be represented, declaring that above seventy people had agreed to sacrifice *favour, honour, and profit* to prevent it. Notwithstanding this fulmination, the performances were ordered to go on. That servants might not be kept in the cold, nor induced to tipple in adjacent ale-houses, while they waited for their masters, the humanity of the gentry had provided that the upper-gallery should afford gratis admission to the servants of such persons as were attending the theatre. Yet these spectators, who were admitted, as it were, for nothing, presumed to forbid the entertainment of their masters, because it exposed their own glaring vices. The farce was no sooner begun than the combined footmen commenced a vigorous opposition. It was in vain that their masters commanded them to be silent. Their opposition only seemed to feed the flame, and although the gentlemen in the boxes were quite able to recognise each his own servant, and to call him to account, it was not till after a vigorous battle, in which the servants were completely overpowered by their masters, and then thrust out of their gallery for ever, that peace was restored, and the play, which has ever since been a favourite in Edinburgh, allowed to proceed with the usual regularity and quietness.—LIFE OF W. H. MURRAY.

QUICK COMPOSITION.

IN the year 1766, Mr Barthelemon composed his first Italian serious opera, entitled *Pelopida*, which he presented at the Opera-house, and it was received with uncommon success and applause. Garrick hearing of his success, paid him a visit, unasked and unexpected, one morning, and asked him if he could set *English words to music*. He repiled, he thought he could. Garrick called for pen and paper, and wrote the words of a song to be introduced in *The Country Girl*, and to be sung by Dodd, in the character of Sparkish. While the Roscius was writing the words, Barthelemon, looking over his shoulder, *set the song!* Garrick gave him the song, and said, "There, my friend, there is my song." Barthelemon instantly replied, "There, sir, there is the music for it!!"

CAPTAIN O'CALLAGHAN.

DURING the fracas occasioned by this *ci-devant* actor's being confined on bread and water, some one was expatiating to Hume, the member, on the hardship of his case. "Think, my dear Sir," said the complainant; "he has nothing but dry bread." "Well," said Hume, "I suppose he has as much of that as he pleases?" "Oh, yes," was the reply. "Well, then," said the M.P., "he has as much *bread* as to him seems *meet*."

AN EARLY CAST OF THE "HEART OF MID-LOTHIAN."

"THEATRE-ROYAL, EDINBURGH.

This Evening, December 16, 1822, will be performed the National Drama of

THE HEART OF MID-LOTHIAN.

John, Duke of Argyle,	Mr Jones.
George Staunton,	Mr Calcraft.
John Dumbie,	Mr Mackay.
David Deans,	Mr Faulkner.
Saddletree,	Mr Boddie.
Reuben Butler,	Mr Denham.
Mr Sharpitlaw,	Mr Mason.
Rasper,	Mr Miller.
Donald,	Mr Power.
James,	Mr Hillyard.
Serjeant of the Guard,	Mr Aikin.
Town-Guard,	Messrs Dow, Mowat, &c.
James Ratcliffe,	Mr Duff.
Black Frank,	Mr Murray.
Tyburn Tam,	Mr Bland.
Queen of England,	Mrs Renaud.
Jeanie Deans,	Mrs H. Siddons.
Effie Deans,	Miss Eyre.
Mrs Glass,	Mrs Nicol.
Betty,	Miss M. Nicoll.
Margery Murdochson,	Mrs Eyre.
Madge Wildfire,	Miss Nicol."

MRS POWELL.

WHEN Mr Boaden had read his unsuccessful drama of "Aurelio and Miranda," in the green-room, he observed, that he knew nothing so terrible as reading a piece before such a critical audience. Mrs Powell, the actress, who was present, said she knew one thing much more terrible. "What can that be?" demanded the author. "To be obliged," said she, "to sit and hear it."

MRS SIDDONS IN EDINBURGH.

Although our space is much limited at present, it would be unpardonable were we to overlook the first appearance of Mrs Siddons on the stage of Edinburgh. The admirable performances of this gifted woman had drawn upon her the admiration of all classes of the people, both in England and Ireland. It is not to be wondered at, therefore, that the learned *savans* of the capital of Scotland were longing to behold this wonderful goddess of tragedy. For the purpose of inducing her to visit Edinburgh, a committee of noblemen and gentlemen made up a purse of the value of £200 to be presented to her, as an addition to what was agreed upon by Mr Jackson. The following is the supposed result, in a pecuniary view, of this first visit to Edinburgh :—

Half of the house (deducting expenses) for nine nights	£467	7	7
Committee's purse	200	0	0
Benefit, at raised prices	180	0	0
Presents, plate, gold—tickets, &c., &c.	120	0	0
Making a total sum of	£967	7	7

which was looked upon, at that time, as something quite enormous.

The sensation produced in Edinburgh by Mrs Siddons' first visit was tremendous, and the crowds that assembled on the occasion have never since been equalled. It is a well-known fact that porters slept on the street on bundles of straw, in order to be close to the box-office on its being opened for the disposal of places, and thus have an opportunity of securing tickets for their employers. On the first evening of performance, immense crowds besieged the doors to take their chance of gaining admittance, and, we believe, the line of carriages engaged in setting down the box company extended half-way along Princes Street. On the first evening of her performing, the house was densely packed—every available corner from which a glimpse of the stage could be seen, or a word from the performer be heard, being occupied. When the lady entered in view of the audience, a silence deep as death was her only welcome. This continued for some time, until at last one individual in the gallery became roused by the almost superhuman grandeur of the acting, gave vent to his admiration, by exclaiming at the conclusion of one of her well-known bursts of passionate feeling—"that's no bad though." This homely exclamation, acting as a charm, at once dissolved the lethargy of the audience, and peal upon peal of applause reverberated through the house, acting, no doubt, as a great charm to the almost wounded feelings of the great actress, who always declared that there was nothing so necessary to the actor or actress as the applause of the audience, which served to give them a brief respite of breathing time, to recruit their lost strength, and recover their wonted energies.—LIFE OF MURRAY.

PUFF DIRECT.

A FRENCH dramatist devised a singular method of alluring the public to the representation of his pieces. On the day for which any of them was announced, he set out in the morning, went through all the streets and squares of Paris, stopping at those places where the play bills were usually posted, and when five or six persons had been collected, he would cry at once in a vehement tone, "Faith, the French will be treated with an excellent piece to-night—I'll be there for one." This peregrination was then continued in the same manner, and its object became, in some measure, successful.

ON MR JONES OF COVENT GARDEN.

NATURE amused herself one day
With modelling a man of clay;
Pleased with the figure she had form'd,
With life his senseless breast she warm'd;
Placed in his hand the lively keys
Of humour and the power to please;
Set sense and reason on their inmost thrones,
Finish'd her task, and call'd the mixture *Jones.*
　　　　　　　　　　　　W. L——G.

A CURIOUS PLAY-BILL.—"ROB ROY," FOR THE LAST TIME IN EDINBURGH!!!

"This Present Evening, Tuesday, April 25, 1848, will be performed, for the LAST TIME IN EDINBURGH, the celebrated National Opera, in Three Acts, entitled
ROB ROY.

Rob Roy Macgregor, by Mr Edmund Glover.
Sir Frederick Vernon, by Mr Ray—Rashleigh Osbaldistone, by Mr Wyndham.
Francis Osbaldistone, by Mr W. H. Eburne, in which character he will sing 'My Love is Like a Red Red Rose'—'Auld Langsyne'—'Macgregor's Gathering.'
And, with Miss Coveney, the Duets of
'Though you Leave me now in Sorrow'—and 'Forlorn and Broken-Hearted.'
Dougal by Mr Josephs—Captain Thornton by Mr Weekley.
Major Galbraith by Mr Murray—Mr Owen by Mr Lloyd.
Bailie Nicol Jarvie by Mr Mackay, being his Last Appearance in that Character in this City.
M'Stuart by Mr Honey—Sergeant by Mr Henry.
Hamish by Mr Carroll—Jobson by Mr Vandrey—Robert by Master Josephs.
Saunders Wylie by Mr Freeman—Andrew Fairservice by Mr C. Lloyds.
Helen Macgregor by Miss Cleaver—Hostess by Mrs Josephs.
Jean M'Alpine by Miss Nicol—Mattie by Miss H. Coveney.
Diana Vernon by Miss Coveney, in which character she will sing 'A Highland Lad my Love was Born'—and a Favourite Ballad.

In the Course of the Evening, Mr Mackay will bid Farewell to his kind Friends and Patrons.

The whole to conclude with, for the LAST TIME IN EDINBURGH, the National Drama, entitled
CRAMOND BRIG.
James, King of Scotland, by Mr Wilson, in which character he will sing the National Ballad of
'The Flowers of the Forest,' and Sir Walter Scott's Ballad of 'The Young Lochinvar.'
Jock Howieson by Mr Mackay, being his Last Appearanc in that Character in this City."

STUDY YOUR NEIGHBOUR'S PART.

In the course of repeatedly reflecting on the part of Romeo, and desirous of attaining to as great perfection as possible in the representation of it, it occurred to Mr Kemble, that in that passage where Romeo in his despair approaches the house of the Apothecary, there had prevailed a great misconception as to the right manner of delivering it. Romeo says:—

"And if a man did need a poison now,
Whose sale is present death in Mantua,
Here lives a caitiff wretch would sell it him;
* * * * * * *
As I remember, this should be the house.
Being holiday, the beggar's shop is shut.
What, ho! Apothecary!"

As the passage had been always hitherto spoken, the player raised his voice in the "what, ho! Apothecary?" to the pitch of "milk below, maids!" Now, reasoned Mr Kemble, could anything be more absurd? A man with all the marks of deep despair, is seen looking about for an apothecary's shop; he is in search of some subtile poison, which it is death in this apothecary to sell; and yet, as if he wanted all the world to witness the purchase, he bawls out with stentorian lungs, "What ho, Apothecary!" Nothing, as Mr Kemble thought, could be more out of character; so he resolved to go a different way to work. On his next representation of Romeo, when he came to the words, "As I remember this should be the house," he lowered his voice to the meditative muttering of some midnight prowler; then in a side whisper, told us, that "Being holiday, the beggar's shop was shut," and at length, in a low sepulchral tone, uttered the magic words, "What ho! Apothecary!"

Thus far all was well; but unfortunately for Mr Kemble's new and rational improvement, Shakespeare happens to have thought differently on the subject; and no sooner had Romeo uttered in this low tone, the words, "What, ho! Apothecary!" than Mr Apothecary stepped forth and demanded,

"*Who calls so loud?*"

The audience, as may readily be supposed, were instantly struck by the strange incongruity, and burst into a general laugh. Mr Kemble was so disconcerted, that he could scarcely proceed with his part, which he now learnt, by a mortifying exposure, could only be performed well by attending to the part which others have to play with him.

THE WAVERLEY NOVELS—GEORGE THE FOURTH IN THE EDINBURGH THEATRE.

"WHILE the dramas from the *Waverley Novels* pleased everywhere, and drew money to the managers throughout the kingdom, in Scotland, as was likely, they found their strongest hold. *Rob Roy* was produced in Edinburgh with great care in February 1819, and ran for forty-one nights without intermission. It was admirably acted throughout, and introduced to that most critical audience a performer who has never been equalled in his particular line—Charles Mackay. His *Bailie Jarvie* was not acting, it was nature, the man personified in living identity, as if he had sat for the picture, and the author had held him in his eye while drawing it. Liston was the admired of the Londoners, and an admirable artist too. His humour was peculiarly his own, and his *Dominie Sampson* was irresistible; but Mackay was the *Bailie* of Sir Walter Scott, as he himself often most emphatically declared. Perhaps the highest compliment ever paid to an actor was when the Great Unknown, at the dinner of the Edinburgh Theatrical Fund, threw aside his useless incognito, publicly owned himself the author of the works long believed to be his, and proposed the health of Mackay, in his character of the *Bailie*, in the following terms:—'I would fain dedicate a bumper to the health of one who has represented several of those characters of which I have endeavoured to give the skeleton, with a truth and liveliness for which I may well be grateful. I beg leave to propose the health of my friend *Bailie Nicol Jarvie*; and I am sure when the author of *Waverley* and *Rob Roy* drinks to *Nicol Jarvie*, it will be received with the just applause to which that gentleman has always been accustomed.' The talents of Mackay were by no means confined to his representation of exclusively national characters. In *Dominie Sampson, Cuddie Headrig, Caleb Balderstone, Dalgetty, Richie Moniplies, Jock Howieson*, &c., &c., he was far beyond any of his contemporaries, and, in a large range of miscellaneous parts, equal to many in the foremost rank. I have seen him play *Rolamo*, in *Clari*, *Old Dornton* in *The Road to Ruin*, and others of that cast, with a power and pathos which everybody acknowledged. I feel happy at an opportunity of bearing my feeble testimony to the merits of an old friend and confederate; and should these pages meet his eye, he will, I am sure, be pleased to find that I have not forgotten the days of 'auld lang syne,' or the many reminiscences of what occurred when we dressed in 'propinquity' in the same room. I introduced him to the Dublin audience; and although (as, I grieve to say, they seldom do) they did not fill the theatre, they felt his excellence, and applauded him to the echo. He has retired, happily, from the anxious avocations of theatrical drudgery, and is, I trust, what I always predicted he would be, 'a warm little man.' The last remaining of that 'ould stock' is my first worthy employer and manager, William Murray, to whom I must, with an early opportunity, dedicate an exclusive leaf, which he is well worthy of, and which, I trust, he will take as a tribute of old friendship. He, too, is about to retire (I wish I was!) and he leaves no actor like himself behind, in a long range of the most opposite characters.

"There was, in the Edinburgh Theatre, at the time I have been alluding to, an actor, by name Denham, now dead, but who deserves to be remembered. I saw him first in a small country theatre at Kelso, and recommended him strongly to Mr Murray, who engaged him at a trifling salary on my showing, but soon promoted him when he discovered his merit. His *Dandie Dinmont* and *Mucklebacket* were masterly pieces of acting; and his *King James*, in *The Fortunes of Nigel*, delighted the author almost as much as the *Bailie Jarvie* of Mackay. It was unique, one of those unexpected coincidences you never dream of, and greatly assisted by a natural thickness of utterance, a sort of Northumbrian, or Border burr (which Sir Walter Scott himself had), in exact keeping with the physical peculiarities of the British Solomon. Neither let poor old Duff be forgotten, who has so lately 'shuffled off his mortal coil,' and whose *Dougal Creature* was equally commended by the same high authority. Perhaps he wanted but the right opportunity, at the right moment, to have made him a great man. The curtain has fallen, and no human reasoning can now decide the question; but that he had talent of a high order, and in a varied line, is unquestionable. Why it was permitted to waste itself in obscurity and indigence, and to be extinguished, in the winter of life, in utter helplessness, we know not, and have no right to inquire, but all, if they choose, may deduce from thence a salutary lesson. I met him first in Edinburgh when I joined that company in 1819. Everybody said he was a clever man; all he did was done like an artist. I saw George the Fourth applaud his *Dougal* warmly. I left him in Edinburgh in 1824, and I found him again in neglect and obscurity, discharged from the Haymarket, in London, in 1830. I was then mustering forces for my first campaign in Dublin; he enlisted under my banners, and never left them until he received the final summons of a more imperative commander.

"When George the Fourth visited Edinburgh, in 1822, he selected *Rob Roy* for the performance on the night of his attending the theatre in state, partly as a national compliment, and partly as a personal distinction to Sir Walter Scott, who had taken much trouble with all the arrangements during the royal sojourn.

"A copy of the bill, with the cast of the play, may not be wholly uninteresting to our theatrical readers:—

'THEATRE-ROYAL, EDINBURGH.

BY COMMAND OF HIS MAJESTY.

This present Tuesday, August 27, 1822, will be performed the National Opera of

ROB ROY MACGREGOR;

OR,

AULD LANGSYNE,

With the original Music and appropriate Scenery, Machinery, Dresses, and Decorations.

Sir Frederick Vernon,	Mr Munro.
Rashleigh Osbaldistone,	Mr Denham.
Francis Osbaldistone,	Mr Huckel.
Captain Thornton,	Mr Murray.
Major Galbraith,	Mr Weekes.
Rob Roy Macgregor Campbell,	Mr Calcraft.
Bailie Nicol Jarvie,	Mr Mackay.
Mr Owen,	Mr Roberts.
Mac Stuart,	Mr Lee.
Dougal,	Mr Duff.
Willie,	Master Hillyard.
Andrew,	Mr Aitken.
Lancel,	Mr Stanley.

Sergeant,	Mr Hillyard.
Saunders Willie,	Mr Power.
Helen Macgregor,	Mrs Renaud.
Martha,	Miss J. Nicol.
Mattie,	Miss Nicol.
Hostess,	Mrs Mackay.
Jean M'Alpine,	Mrs Nicol.
Diana Vernon (for this night only),	Mrs H. Siddons.'

"There was no after-piece; the doors opened at six, and the performances were to commence at eight, or as soon after as the King arrived, who was always punctual. The crowd began to assemble with the dawn of day; at twelve it came on to rain, and rained incessantly until six; but 'no thought was there of dastard flight;' money was offered for places in the throng, and indignantly refused; the 'serried phalanx' maintained their array until the appointed hour, and within a few minutes after, the pit was densely packed; then arose from saturated garments a thick mist of damp and vapour, through which gas illuminations were but dimly seen, and which had scarcely dispersed when His Majesty entered his state-box. We recollect looking out from the window of our dressing-room on that wet and wearied crowd, impatient and worn out, and saying to ourselves, as the highwayman did on his way to Tyburn, and knowing we were to act the leading part in a very different sort of drama, 'You need not hurry, there'll be no fun till I come.'

"Of the performers whose names appear in the bill we have copied not more than eight are now alive.

"The play of *Rob Roy*, up to this date, has been acted in Edinburgh nearly four hundred times, and in the provincial theatres of Scotland more than one thousand. I remember seeing the five hundredth representation announced in a playbill of Ryder's at Perth, dated as far back as 1829.

"The week before the arrival of the King all Scotland poured into Edinburgh. It was impossible to walk the streets without being jostled off the curbstones; but, like sensible and well ordered lieges, as they are, they crowded the theatre nightly. In six evenings, with no auxiliary attraction, above £1000 was taken to the two old national and worn-out dramas of *Rob Roy* and the *Heart of Mid-Lothian*. Then came Edmund Kean, who had been engaged long before there was any intimation or idea of a royal visit, and the houses, if possible, were fuller still. The great tragedian, then in the full zenith of his fame and powers, was naturally much chagrined that one of his plays was not selected on the night of the royal command, and expected *Macbeth*. I thought he would have chosen to study *Rob Roy* for the occasion, which he had an undoubted right to do if he pleased, but I was not sorry to find he had no such intention. He was impressed with a most unfounded notion that the sovereign was personally hostile to him, and said to me, in conversation on the subject, with epigrammatic bitterness, 'I am a greater man than ever I expected to be—I have a king for my enemy!'"—*Dublin University Magazine*.

QUIN.

A YOUNG fellow, who fancied himself possessed of talents, offered himself to this gentleman, who desired a specimen of his abilities. After he had rehearsed, in a wretched manner, some part in tragedy, Quin asked him, with a contemptuous sneer, whether he had performed in comedy. The young fellow answered, he had done the part of Abel, in *The Alchymist*. "You! you mistake, boy," replied Quin; "it was the part of *Cain* you acted, for I am certain you murdered *Abel!*"

PUNCH AND THE DRAMA.

ON the night of the celebration of the Jubilee in honour of Shakespeare, a supper was given to all the performers. At the head of the table, sat Messrs Kemble and "*the great creatures;*" at the foot, Messrs Simmons and *the little* creatures. And, to be in keeping, the upper tables groaned beneath Champaigne, Bucellas, Sherry, &c., whilst the lower ones supported plain *punch*.—Mr Faucit Saville remarked, with much wit and poignancy, "That it was a degradation to the regular drama to introduce *Punch* on such an occasion."

JOHN KEMBLE'S FAREWELL TO THE EDINBURGH STAGE.

"As the worn war-horse, at the trumpet's sound,
Erects his mane, and neighs, and paws the ground—
Disdains the ease his generous lord assigns,
And longs to rush on the embattled lines,
So I, your plaudits ringing on mine ear,
Can scarce sustain to think our parting near;
To think my scenic hour for ever past,
And that these valued plaudits are my last.
Why should we part, while still some powers remain,
That in your service strive not yet in vain?
Cannot high zeal the strength of youth supply,
And sense of duty fire the fading eye;
And all the wrongs of age remain subdued
Beneath the burning glow of gratitude?
Ah, no! the taper, wearing to its close,
Oft for a space in fitful lustre glows;
But all too soon the transient gleam is past,
It cannot be renew'd, and will not last;
Even duty, zeal, and gratitude, can wage
But short-lived conflict with the frosts of age.
Yes! it were poor, remembering what I was,
To live a pensioner on your applause,
To drain the dregs of your endurance dry,
And take, as alms, the praise I once could buy;
Till every sneering youth around enquires,
'Is this the man who once could please our sires?'
And scorn assumes compassion's doubtful mien,
To warn me off from the encumber'd scene.
This must not be;—and higher duties crave,
Some space between the theatre and the grave,
That, like the Roman in the Capitol,
I may adjust my mantle ere I fall:
My life's brief act in public service flown,
The last, the closing scene, must be my own.

"Here, then, adieu! while yet some well-graced parts
May fix an ancient favourite in your hearts,

Not quite to be forgotten, even when
You look on other actors, younger men ;
And if your bosoms own this kindly debt
Of old remembrance, how shall mine forget—
O, how forget!—how oft I hither came
In anxious hope, how oft return'd with fame!
How oft around your circle this weak hand
Has waved immortal Shakespeare's magic wand,
Till the full burst of inspiration came,
And I have felt, and you have fann'd the flame!
By mem'ry treasured, while her reign endures,
Those hours must live—and all their charms are yours.

"O favour'd Land! renown'd for arts and arms,
For manly talent, and for female charms,
Could this full bosom prompt the sinking line,
What fervent benedictions now were thine!
But my last part is play'd, my knell is rung,
When e'en your praise falls faltering from my tongue;
And all that you can hear, or I can tell,
Is—Friends and Patrons, hail, and FARE YOU WELL." *

Walter Scott.

QUIN.

This gentleman had, on one occasion, performed the part of *Falstaff*, for the benefit of his friend Ryan. His success on that occasion induced the latter to solicit the same favour some time after: the application produced the following laconic answer from Quin:—

"I would play for you if I could, but will not *whistle* for you. I have will'd you a thousand pounds. If you want money, you can have it, and save my executors trouble.

"Bath, March 1st. "JAMES QUIN."

---

* "Mr Kemble delivered these lines with exquisite beauty, and with an effect that was evidenced by the tears and sobs of many of the audience. His own emotions were very conspicuous. When his farewell was closed, he lingered long on the stage, as if unable to retire. The house again stood up, and cheered him with the waving of hats and long shouts of applause. At length, he finally retired, and, in so far as regards Scotland, the curtain dropped upon his professional life for ever."—*The Sale Room.*

TONY BRUN'S SALT FISH.

Tony Brun, an erratic comedian, with more ambition than ability, was no less remarkable for his singular simplicity, than extreme fondness for angling. When he was member of the Liverpool theatre, he laid one evening several lines in a stream near the town, in hopes of procuring an excellent dinner for the next day. In the course of the night, a theatrical wag, belonging to the same company, went to the place, drew up his hooks, and on some of them fixed *red herrings*, and on others *sparrows*, carefully placing them again in the former situation. Early in the morning, Tony went with a friend to secure his expected prize, and drew up the red herrings; upon which he said, "Before God! here are herrings! and, upon my faith, *ready pickled*, too!" Proceeding farther, he drew the sparrows on shore: after examining them attentively he exclaimed, "God bless my soul! this is indeed very surprising! I don't wonder at catching the *red herrings*, because they were in their own element, but I really never before thought that birds lived in *water!* I should as soon have expected to have shot *fish* in the *air!* But I will take care and not be disappointed a second time, by laying my lines here for *fresh fish!*"

MR HERBERT.

During a pantomime, at Sheffield, in which he performed the *Clown, Harlequin*, disguised as a watchman, at the door of a night-cellar, which opened by a trap, stood ready to strike him on the head when he appeared, for which purpose a wooden head was customarily provided. Unluckily, at the moment, the block was missing, when Herbert in the bustle, and zealous for the cause, and thoughtless of the danger, used his own, which was instantly accosted with so severe a blow, that he fell back through the stage. A momentary consternation prevailed, in the idea that he was inevitably killed; but their fears were soon dispelled, by hearing him bawl out, "I'm a dead man! he's killed me; he's killed me!" and running on the stage, went through his character as pleasantly as ever.

GEORGE FREDERICK COOKE IN AMERICA.

A GENTLEMAN told Cooke, that Mr Maddison, the President of the United States, purposed to come from Washington to Baltimore to see him act. "If he does, I'll be damn'd if I play before him. What! I! George Frederick Cooke, who have acted before the Majesty of Great Britain—I play before your *Yankee President!* No—I'll go forward to the audience, and say, 'Ladies and gentlemen, the *King of the Yankee Doodles* has come to see me act.—Me,—me, George Frederick Cooke, who have stood before my Royal Master, George the Third, and received his imperial approbation! and shall I exert myself to play before one of his rebellious subjects, who arrogates kingly state in defiance of his master.' No, it is degradation enough to play before *rebels*, but I'll not go on for the amusement of a *King of Rebels*, the *contemptible King of the Yankee Doodles*."

A THEATRICAL RECOLLECTION.

THE Hawthorn, who had by no means a bad voice, unfortunately lisped pretty strongly, and, in consequence, he no sooner commenced singing, than the audience evinced their disapprobation in sounds most discordant to an actor's ears—a sound professionally said to proceed from "the big bird," (the goose); but Hawthorn, "good easy man," continued his song, and the audience their opposition. He bore it "with a patient shrug." *He* sang and *they* hissed, till at length his patience and forbearance being exhausted, he stepped forward, and addressed the audience thus:—"Ladieth and thentlemen, I am very thorry to find you don't approve of my thinging and that you hith. I athure you I am doing the very betht I can for your amuthement; and all I thay ith, that hith ath long ath you pleath, we have no one elth in our company to play the part; and I have been very thukthethful in it in platheth of greater magnitude than thith. No dithrethpect intended to you."

Printed by Libri Plureos GmbH in Hamburg, Germany